I'M OFFENDED

Copyright © 2023 Brad Gosse

I have over 100 humor books and several strange coloring books available on Amazon.

My humor books cover a wide range of topics and styles, from dumb jokes and puns to satirical takes on current events. Whatever your sense of humor, you'll find something to love or hate in my collection.

And for those who want to tap into their creative side, my strange coloring books offer unique and unconventional designs for you to color in and make your own. These books are perfect for relaxing after a long day, or for getting in touch with your inner artist.

So don't wait any longer to add some laughter and creativity to your life. Check out my other books on Amazon today!

Here are just a few...

books.bradgosse.com

I'M OFFENDED BY THE SUN

IT SPOILS MY FUN

I'M OFFENDED BY THE MOON

IT'S UP TOO SOON

I'M OFFENDED BY THE AIR

IT'S EVERYWHERE, AND IT'S NOT FAIR

I'M OFFENDED BY THE SEA

IT'S FAR TOO WET, YOU MUST AGREE

I'M OFFENDED BY YOUR SMILE

IT CRAMPS MY STYLE

I'M OFFENDED BY YOUR FROWN

YOU LOOK LIKE A SAD CLOWN

I'M OFFENDED, IT'S TRUE

BY EVERYTHING, ESPECIALLY YOU

BUT MOST OF ALL, TO BE CLEAR

I'M OFFENDED THAT WE'RE EVEN HERE

AND SO I SIT, IN DARK DISDAIN

OFFENDED BY MY VERY BRAIN

IN THE END, IT'S PLAIN TO SEE

THE THING THAT OFFENDS MOST IS ME

MIKE HUNT

SMELLS LIKE FISH

Clap along with Mike Hunt. This book is filled with hilarious double entendres. You know what it's about. Don't make me spell it out for you. This book is cheap as balls. Like your mom.

Every girl, and some guys want my big black hawk. This book teaches you why big black hawks matter.

ALL THE GIRLS LOVE
MY BIG BLACK HAWK

CUCUMBER CURTIS

Can't come to dinner. Your mom has other plans for this innocent little vegetable.

GLUCK GLUCK 3000

Sex Robots are the new wave of the future in sexual entertainment. In fact, they're already in the process of being built. Catering to the needs of lonely men and women, these bots will soon be ubiquitous.

RACE WARS

Black, car, white car, and yellow car too.

STD'S & YOU

Learning From The Animals At The Zoo

GET YOUR VERY OWN DEAD BABIES BOOKS AND MERCHANDISE

Dead Babies are the hottest thing this Christmas season. Every kid wants a book, sticker and shower curtain. Collect them all or trade with your friends. Digital (NFT) collectables also available.

Order while supplies last.

BOOKS

Satisfaction Guaranteed

CONJOINED TWINS
Where Does One End and The Other Begin?

What if one can swim and the other can not? Can just one of them become an astronaut? How often do they need a diaper change? If they grew 100 feet tall wouldn't that be strange? Are they a by-product of nuclear radiation? Have they ever been left outside a fire station?

LEARN ABOUT INBREEDING WITH DONKEYBEAR

Are your parents cousins or siblings? This book will teach you all about inbreeding. You can learn along with Donkeybear. He's hearing about it for the first time.

MOM RUNS TRAINS
On The Weekend With Dad's Friends

It's career day at school. And I get to present. I'm so proud of my mom. And the weekends she's spent. Learning to run trains.

SANTAS LIL HUMPER
SAVES CHRISTMAS

Santa crashes in the Middle East and Rudolf is dead. Only a strange camel can save Christmas now.

BAA BAA BLACK SHEEP
Deals With Another Routine Stop

Baa baa black sheep please step out of the car. Yes sir yes sir please know I'm unarmed. Do you know why I stopped you today?. "Because of the fur color I display?". You match the description of a suspect I seek. Funny it's the 4th time to happen this week. I profiled you because you are black. And you drive a Mercedes which seems kinda whack.

Dad left your mom broke. Now she's faced with the harsh reality of not having enough money. But don't worry she has a plan to get back on her feet.

Does Anyone Know Whatever Happened To
MURDER HORNETS

Remember Murder Hornets? Whatever happened to them? We dive deeply into the terror phenomenon that never came to be. 2020 had so many bigger things, so Murder Hornets were forgotten.

What can pimps and divorce lawyers teach children, about money and luck? This book tells the story of outdated wisdom and harsh truths.

Cockroach-baby smells really musky. Centipede baby was sewn from human skin. Squid-fish lives deep down in the sea. Flesh-eating ladybug is super scary. Bearded baby was born this hairy.

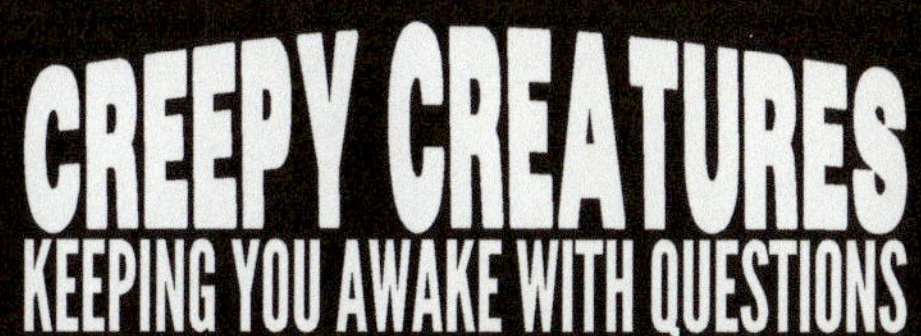

SOFA KING

KLUKEE
The Plant Based Chicken

OURS BABY
The Only Child Your Step Mom Loves

Your stepmom wants one thing from your dear old dad. Viable sperm and an empty house. Pack your bags it's time to grow up.

MOMMY GOT A DUI

Your mom has secrets. She hides her drinking from you… Until now. Mommy can't drive you to school and you're going to have to learn the bus routes.

INSOMNIAC & FRIENDS
The Clowns That Put You To Sleep

Yeetyeet likes to watch you sleep. Pickles under your bed he creeps. Switchblade eats your favorite stuffies. Pedo lures you away with puppies. Shifty plans to collect your teeth. Twisty smells your hair while you sleep. Clammy lives inside his van. Hank once had to kill a man. Tooty smells your dirty socks. Busby laughs at electric shocks. Twinkles spends the night robbing graves. Fappy keeps a few human slaves.

MY RACIST GRAN

WHY DADDY HITS MOMMY

A Kids Guide To Understanding Alcoholism

DEAD BABIES
COLORING BOOKS

TRIGGERED
Kids Guide To Cancel Culture

Easily offended is the new trend. People act outraged. Be careful, you might lose your job. Even though nobody is responsible for the feelings of others.

OK BOOMER

Boomer always complains at the store. But it was on sale yesterday!! When yesterday's special isn't available anymore. You shouldn't be such a slut. Boomer gives unsolicited advice. This smart phone is dumber than dirt. Boomer always struggles with his device. Boomer demands your supervisor.

CANDIS NUTS
Come In The Morning Each Day

CINNAMON

A horse forced into the sex trade.

DON'T BATHE WITH UNCLE JOE
Setting Boundaries With Adults
Uncle Joe lost his job. For misconduct in the workplace. He's coming to stay with us. You're going to have to learn to avoid his hands and more importantly. NEVER bathe with uncle Joe.

THIRST TRAPS
Why Moms Phone Keeps Blowing Up

DADDY'S A SIMP
Don't Expect Much Inheritance

HUMPTY DUMPTY
Discovers Workplace Misconduct